GUITAR METHOD 1
BY
PETER VOGL

An excellent method for learning note reading on the
acoustic or electric guitar.

INTRODUCTION

Guitar Method 1 is designed to help all guitarists learn to read traditional music notation. This includes beginners as well as accomplished guitarists that play by ear and would like to learn to read music. This clear step by step method represents the first major innovation in note reading books in the last 50 years and draws upon the extensive teaching experience of one of the world's leading guitar instructors. The method teaches you practical songs and scales that are currently used today which will enable you to apply what you have learned to the songs that you want to play. The two CDs that come with this method are recorded by top studio musicians and will enable you to hear every exercise and example in this course. In addition, there are over 60 play along jam tracks that will let you play along with a full band, which not only is fun but will help you perfect your timing and ability to play with others. These tracks will also let you practice and perform for student recitals.

THE AUTHOR

Peter Vogl, the author of this book, has been a professional performer and teacher in the Atlanta area for over twenty years. He was raised in Michigan and went to college at the University of Georgia, where he majored in classical guitar performance. He also did post graduate work at James Madison University. Peter has set up and directed six different schools of music in the Atlanta area and currently works at Jan Smith Studios as a session player and guitar instructor. He has written several instructional courses including *Introduction to Blues Guitar Book & DVD*, *Introduction to Rock Guitar Book & DVD*, *The Guitarist's Tablature Book*, *The Guitarist's Chord Book*, *The Guitarist's Scale Book*, *The Guitarist's Lick Book & DVD*, *The Guitarist's Music Theory Book*, and the *Let's Jam! CD Series* (eight different jam along CDs).

WATCH & LEARN PRODUCTS REALLY WORK

For over 25 years, Watch & Learn has revolutionized music instructional courses by developing well thought out, step by step instructional methods that were tested for effectiveness on beginners before publication. Each course is developed by top instructors that actively teach and are in touch with the current needs of students. Coupled with the consistent high standards of Watch & Learn, this has dramatically improved the success and enjoyment of beginning musicians and has set the standard for music instruction today. This easy to understand course will help you tremendously on your journey to having fun and becoming a well rounded guitarist.

CD COUNTERS

The CD counters are included in this book to show where each exercise is located on the companion CDs. There are two sets of CD markers found in this book. One for the Exercise CD and one for the Songs CD. Use your remote control on the CD player to skip to the track you want.

THE TWO AUDIO CDS

There are two audio CDs with this book. *Disc 1 - Exercises* contains all of the exercises in the book. The audio is mixed with the metronome on the right channel and the guitar on the left channel so you can isolate the metronome if you like. *Disc 2 - Songs* contains all of the songs performed with a live band. There are two versions of each song, one with guitar playing along with the band and a second version with only the band so you can play along.

COMPANION PRODUCTS

Guitarist's Chord Book by Peter Vogl contains over 900 chord diagrams with photos to clearly illustrate each chord. Our *Chordfinder System*, using icons and letters, makes finding chords easy. It also contains *Peter's Picks*, goodies from Peter's bag of tricks to give you new sounds, shapes, and inspiration for song arrangements. A must for every guitarist. $9.95

Guitarist's Scale Book by Peter Vogl is a complete scale encyclopedia with over 400 scales and modes. It contains scale diagrams with notation and tablature for each scale and tips on how and when to use each scale. Our *Scalefinder System*, using icons and letters, makes finding scales easy. $9.95

Guitarist's Music Theory Book by Peter Vogl is a clear, concise, easy to understand music theory book for guitarists. This book with audio CD is designed for beginners to experts and teaches the logic or rules of music used by the top professionals.
Book with audio CD $14.95

FOLLOWUP PRODUCTS

Acoustic Rock Guitar Primer by Peter Vogl is designed for the raw beginner who wants to learn rock & roll on the acoustic guitar. It starts with the basics, proper hand position, tuning, & scales and progresses to chords and strumming, arpeggios, and power chords. Play along with a full band on the audio CD or DVD.
Book with audio CD $14.95 DVD $9.95

These products are available at your local music store or send a check including $5.00 shipping and handling to the following address:

Watch & Learn, Inc.
1882 Queens Way
Atlanta, GA 30341
800-416-7088

TABLE OF CONTENTS

	Page	CD1 1	CD2 1-2 Songs

SECTION 1 - GETTING STARTED

	Page	CD1	CD2 Songs
The Guitar	1		
Tuning The Guitar	2	1	
Relative Tuning	3		
Holding The Guitar	4		
The Pick	5		
Right Hand Position	6		
Left Hand Position	7		
What Frets Mean To You	8		

SECTION 2 - THE STAFF, NOTES, AND OPEN STRINGS

	Page	CD1	CD2 Songs
Notes	10		
Rests	11		
The Staff	12		
Time Signature	13		
Ledger Lines	14		
Open 1st, 2nd and 3rd Strings	15-16	2-6	
Song 1 - Openings	16		1-2
Open 6th, 5th, and 4th Strings	17	7-11	
Song 2 - Minor Melody	18		3-4

SECTION 3 - 1ST POSITION NOTES

	Page	CD1	CD2 Songs
Notes on the First String	20-21	12-18	
Notes on the Second String	22-24	19-24	
Song 3 - Onto Blues	23		5-6
Song 4 - Basically A Minor	24		7-8
Song 5 - The Pedal	24		9-10
Notes on the Third String	25-28	25-29	
The Pick Up	26	30	
Song 6 - Chord Tones	27		11-12
Song 7 - Aura Lee	27		13-14
Song 8 - 8 Bars of Blues	28		15-16
Song 9 - When the Saints...	28		17-18
Notes on the Fourth String	29-31	31-35	
Song 10 - Ring Tones	30		19-20
Ties	30		

Song 11 - Will the Circle	31		21-22
Song 12 - Waltz in G	31		23-24
Notes on the 5th String	32-35	36-40	
C Major and A Minor Scales	33	41-42	
Eighth Notes	34	43-44	
Song 13 - Major Scale Melody	35		25-26
Song 14 - Straight Eight Blues	35		27-28
Notes on the 6th String	36-37	45-49	
1st Endings and 2nd Endings	37		
Song 15 - 3/4 Time Arpeggios	37		29-30
The E minor Pentatonic Scale	38	50	
Song 16 - Hold for Two	38		31-32

SECTION 4 - SHARPS, FLATS, AND KEY SIGNATURES

Sharps, Flats, Naturals	40	51-53	
The Chromatic Scale	41	54-55	
Song 17 - Accidental Boogie	42		33-34
Dotted Notes	43	56-57	
Song 18 - Majorly Blue	44		35-36
Song 19 - Catalonian Song	44		37-38
Key of G, C, and F	45-46	58-60	
Song 20 - Careless Love	47		39-40
Song 21 - Bouree	47		41-43
Song 22 - Minuet in G	48		44-46
Song 23- High Pedal In G	48		47-48

SECTION 5 - HARMONY AND CHORDS

Chords and Harmony	50	61-65	
Song 24 - Chord Play	51		49-50
Song 25 - D Melody	52		51-52
Song 26 - Arpeggiation	53		53-54
Song 27 - Wayfaring Stranger	54		55-56
Song 28 - G Blues	55		57-58
Playing B on the 3rd String	55		
Song 29 - Kemp's Jig	56		59
Song 30 - Cascade in E	57		60-61
Song 31 - E Blues Double Stops	58		62-63

SECTION 1
GETTING STARTED

THE GUITAR

Your guitar should be stored in a neutral environment. This means not too cold, not too hot, not too wet, and not too dry. The wood in a guitar is subject to change and will expand or contract in response to it's environment. Too much of any of these things could cause permanent damage. For example, never leave you guitar in your car for long periods of time during summer or winter months. Attics and basements tend to be poor locations for storing a guitar as well.

If you use a strap with your guitar to stand up and play, always keep a hand on the guitar. Straps won't always hold and a guitar falling from that height is never good. You can purchase strap locks to add another level of security, but if the strap itself breaks, the guitar may still fall.

The following photo shows the parts of a steel string guitar..

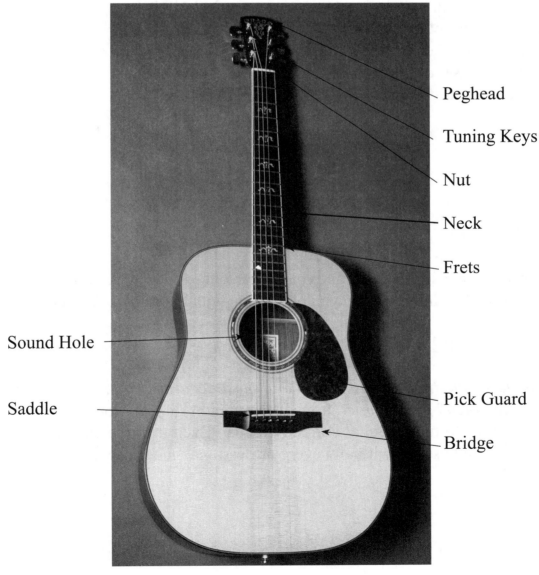

Peghead

Tuning Keys

Nut

Neck

Frets

Sound Hole

Pick Guard

Saddle

Bridge

 Purchase a music stand. People who use one tend to practice up to 30% longer.

1

TUNING THE GUITAR

Before playing the guitar, it must be tuned to standard pitch. If you have a piano at home, it can be used as a tuning source. The following picture shows which note on the piano to tune each open string of the guitar to.

Middle C

E A D G B E

6 5 4 3 2 1

Note: If your piano hasn't been tuned recently, the guitar may not agree perfectly with a pitch pipe or tuning fork. Some older pianos are tuned a half step below standard pitch. In this case, use one of the following methods to tune.

CD OR DVD

It is recommended that you tune your guitar to the CD that accompanies this book so that you will be in tune when you play along with the songs and exercises.

ELECTRONIC TUNER

An electronic tuner is the fastest and most accurate way to tune a guitar. I highly recommend getting one. It may take months or years for a beginner to develop the skills to tune a guitar correctly by ear. Even then the electronic tuner is more precise and used by virtually every professional guitar player.

TIP *Never leave your instrument in a car or trunk during extreme heat or cold.*

RELATIVE TUNING

Relative tuning means to tune the guitar to itself and is used in the following situations:

1. When you do not have an electronic tuner or other source to tune from.
2. When you have only one note to tune from.

In the following example we will tune all of the strings to the 6th string of the guitar, which is an E note.

1. Place the ring finger of the left hand behind the 5th fret of the 6th string to fret the 1st note. Tune the 5th string open (not fretted) until it sounds like the 6th string fretted at the 5th fret.
2. Fret the 5th string at the 5th fret. Tune the 4th string open (not fretted) until it sounds like the 5th string at the 5th fret.
3. Fret the 4th string at the 5th fret. Tune the 3rd string open until it sounds like the 4th string at the 5th fret.
4. Fret the 3rd string at the 4th fret. Tune the 2nd string until it sounds like the 3rd string at the 4th fret.
5. Fret the 2nd string at the 5th fret. Tune the 1st string open until it sounds like the 2nd string at the 5th fret.

Now repeat the above procedure to fine tune the guitar. Until your ear develops, have your teacher or a guitar playing friend check the tuning to make sure it is correct.

The following diagram of the guitar fret board illustrates the above procedure.

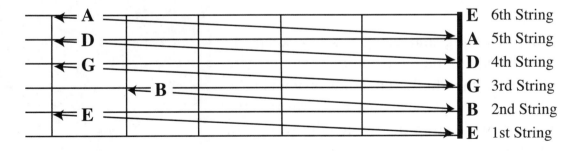

Note - Old dull strings lose their tonal qualities and sometimes tune incorrectly. Check with your teacher or favorite music store to make sure your strings are in good playing condition.

Always keep an extra set of strings in your case.
You never know when you will break one.

HOLDING THE GUITAR

CASUAL POSITION

There are two basic sitting positions for holding the guitar. The first and most common is the casual position. Sit erect with both feet on the floor and the guitar resting on your right thigh. The guitar should be braced against your chest with the right forearm so that the neck of the guitar doesn't move much when you change hand positions.

CLASSICAL POSITION

The second position is the classical position. Sit erect with your right foot on the floor and your left foot elevated on a footstool. The guitar rests on your left leg with the neck elevated. This position allows for a better back position and may make it easier for those who have back pain. It also allows for more freedom of movement of the left arm by raising the guitar neck and removing the left leg as an obstacle.

STANDING POSITION

When standing and using a strap, keep the guitar elevated for better technique, somewhere around waist to chest high, depending on your build. Use a good strap or it may cause discomfort in the shoulders. A wide strap distributes the weight of the guitar better and is recommended.

TIP

Always use a case or gig bag when transporting your instrument from one place to another.

THE PICK

SELECTING THE PICK

When you visit a music store, you will notice that there are almost as many pick styles and shapes as there are guitar players. A pick should feel comfortable in your hand and produce a clear, clean tone when picking or strumming the strings. This is the most popular pick shape.

HOLDING THE PICK

The grip on a pick should provide control while feeling comfortable. The most common way of holding the pick is to curl the right index finger (Figure 1), place the pick in the first joint of the index finger with the point facing straight out (Figure 2), and then place the thumb firmly on the pick with the thumb parallel to the first joint (Figure 3).

Figure 1

Figure 2

Figure 3

Keep many extra picks around. They like to disappear, much like socks.

RIGHT HAND POSITION

Position the right hand so that the pick strikes the strings between the bridge and the fretboard. The top of the right forearm should be braced against the body of the guitar so that the right hand falls into a position towards the center of the sound hole. Do not rest your wrist or palm on the bridge. Too close to the bridge produces a bright tone and too far forward produces a tone that may be too dark. The right hand should be free with no part of the hand or wrist touching the guitar.

Bright   Correct   Too Dark   Wrist Not Resting on Guitar

LEFT HAND FINGERS

The index finger is the first finger, the middle finger is the second finger, the ring finger is the third finger and the pinky is the fourth finger. The thumb is not given a number since it is on the back of the neck.

 TIP *Use a guitar cloth to clean your guitar and wipe it down after you play.*

6

LEFT HAND POSITION

When positioning your left hand on the guitar, pay careful attention to several things. The left elbow should hang freely to the outside of the left leg. Don't let your elbow creep into a position resting on the left leg or more into the body. This will avoid undue stress on the elbow and wrist. The hand itself should be positioned so the fingers can stay in front of the guitar neck.

THUMB POSITION

The thumb placement can vary a little due to hand and body size. Our basic thumb position will be around half way up the back of the guitar neck. This is our *core position*, meaning use this position most of the time. There will be times when we use an elevated thumb position, but this may compromise technique. We will discuss when to do this at a later time. Smaller hands should have an even lower thumb placement. This allows for better stretching and finger dexterity.

WRIST POSITION

The wrist should be below the guitar neck, which is our *wrist core position*.

A guitar should have a set-up every 6 months or so. Check with you local music store for this service.

WHAT FRETS MEAN TO YOU

Frets are the little metal bars on the neck of the guitar. When pressing down on a string in a fret space, the sound of the note comes from the fret in front of the finger (or to the left in the photo below). This is very, very important. What this means is **when we are pressing down any string in any fret, we are not trying to hold the string against the wood of the guitar neck**. (Read above phrase again as reinforcement). We are holding the string down so it touches the fret in front of it.

Finger at front of fret and good position

Finger in back of fret and poor position

CHORD DIAGRAMS

In this book you will find chord diagrams that will help you visualize where fingers should be placed on the guitar. Study the diagram below so that you will understand these diagrams when you see them.

TIP *Once the frets on a guitar have large divots, they need to be replaced. This is called a fret job.*

SECTION 2
THE STAFF, NOTES, AND
OPEN STRINGS

NOTE PARTS

Notes can have several different parts depending on what type of note they are.

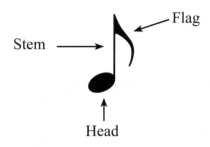

NOTE RHYTHMS

The type of note tells us how many beats to hold it or what rhythm to play. A whole note, which is a hollow note head, typically lasts for four beats or counts. The half note, which has a hollow head and a stem, lasts for two beats. The quarter note, which has a solid head and a stem, lasts for 1 beat. The eighth note has a solid head, a stem and one flag and lasts for half of a beat. (Two eighth notes last the same amount of time as one quarter note). The sixteenth note has a solid head, stem, and two flags. It lasts for a quarter of a beat (Four sixteenth notes lasts the same amount of time as a quarter note).

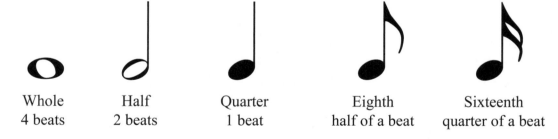

The diagram below shows how many half, quarter, eighth, and sixteenth notes it would take to last the same amount of time as a whole note. Two half notes equal one whole note. Two quarter notes equal one half note. Two eighth notes equal one quarter note. Two sixteenth notes equal one eighth note.

RESTS

When reading music, we also need to know when not to play. Rests tell us how much time to wait before we play again.

THE STAFF

The staff is where we place the notes telling us what pitch to play. The staff is made up of ledger lines and spaces.

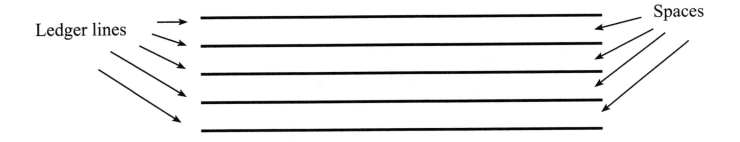

Ledger lines →

Spaces ←

There are several elements added to the staff giving us more information. The clef sign tells us what pitches the lines and spaces represent. When playing guitar we use the treble clef.

Treble Clef

The treble clef sign tells us that the lines and spaces represent specific pitches. The spaces from the bottom up are the pitches F, A, C, E. The lines from the bottom up are E, G, B, D, F.

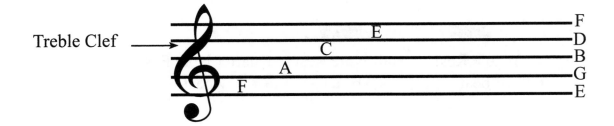

Treble Clef →

BAR LINES

Bar lines are added to the staff to divide it into smaller units called measures or bars. This will make the staff easier to read and it will also tell us information about the rhythms and what notes are accented. Typically we accent the first beat in a measure. We will learn more about this as we learn about time signature.

TIME SIGNATURE

Time signature is a symbol that tells us how many beats are in a measure. There are many time signatures and a few that are used more than others. Below are examples of the most frequently used time signatures.

Four four time means four beats to a measure and the quarter note is the beat.

Two four time means two beats to a measure and the quarter note is the beat.

Three four time means three beats to a measure and the quarter note is the beat.

Common time is another way to say four four time.

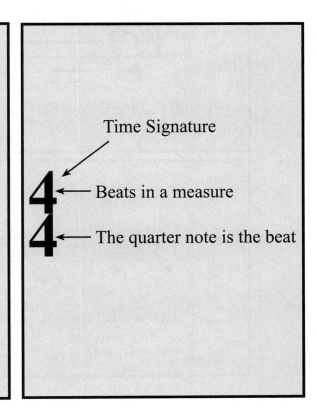

Time Signature

Beats in a measure

The quarter note is the beat

13

NOTES ON THE STAFF

Now we can see what the notes actually look like on the staff. Notes lower on the staff are lower in pitch. Notes higher on the staff are higher in pitch.

Lower Notes Higher Notes

LEDGER LINES

We can go higher or lower than the five lines and spaces that make up the staff by adding extra ledger lines. It is like adding a line to the staff but we use just a small line. The reason we do this is to make the staff easier to read. Otherwise we would need a staff with many lines and spaces.

Ledger Lines Above Staff

Ledger Lines Below Staff

Ledger Lines allow for higher notes

Ledger Lines allow for lower notes

TIP
Heavier gauge strings offer more tone due to their thickness.

OPEN 1ST, 2ND, AND 3RD STRINGS

Here are the notes representing the first three open strings on the guitar. It is important to memorize notes as we introduce them. Otherwise you will have difficulty playing the exercises or advancing your note reading skills.

E - OPEN 1ST STRING   **B - OPEN 2ND STRING**   **G - OPEN 3RD STRING**

Open 1st String   Open 2nd String   Open 3rd String

E   B   G

You will see these symbols throughout this book. The symbol with two prongs pointing downward means use a downstroke with your pick. The V shaped symbol means use a upstroke with your pick. These are suggestions that help you play more smoothly.

Exercise 1

This exercise will help you learn the first three open strings. Remember whole notes last for four beats. In all exercises the pick directions are only suggestions. If playing with fingers (right hand) try alternating the index and middle finger. The most important items to focus on are playing the correct notes and playing in time.

Count: 1 2 3 4

Exercise 2

This exercise demonstrates the open strings and playing half notes. Remember half notes last two beats.

Count: 1 2 3 4

15   **TIP**   *Practice slow and relaxed.*

CD1
5

Exercise 3

In this exercise we are primarily playing quarter notes. A quarter note lasts one beat. Alternate the pick directions. When you are given pick directions for only the first measure, it means you can generally repeat this pattern throughout the exercise or tune.

Count: 1 2 3 4

CD1
6

Exercise 4

This exercise will use a variety of rhythms. Practice playing the first three open strings and playing the correct rhythms.

Count: 1   2   3   4   1   2   3   4   1   2   3   4   1   2   3   4

1   2   3   4   1   2   3   4

CD2
1-2
Songs

OPENINGS

This tune highlights an Em arpeggio. *Arpeggio means to play one note of a chord at a time*. This song and many others in this book have a background track to play along with. One track is an example with melody and background music. Another track is just the background music allowing you to play the melody. There is a four beat click or count off before you are to begin playing. The chords used to accompany each tune are written above the staff.

Count: 1   2   3   4   1   2   3   4

TIP *Guitars should be set up by a luthier if you change gauges of strings.*

16

OPEN 6TH, 5TH AND 4TH STRINGS

Here are the lowest three open strings on the guitar. Memorize them and move on to the next exercise.

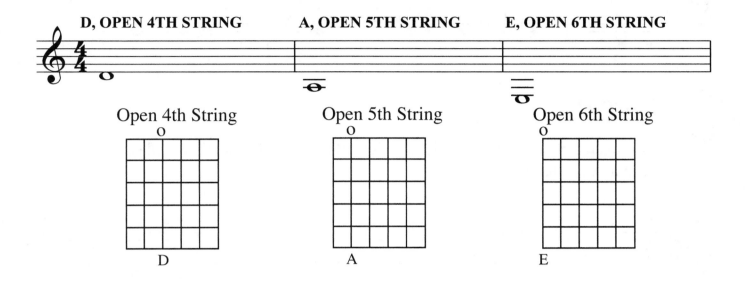

D, OPEN 4TH STRING   **A, OPEN 5TH STRING**   **E, OPEN 6TH STRING**

Open 4th String   Open 5th String   Open 6th String

D   A   E

Exercise 5

This whole note exercise will help you learn the bottom three open strings on the guitar. Practice smoothly and evenly.

Count: 1 2 3 4

Exercise 6

Practice this half note exercise on the lowest three open strings.

Count: 1   2   3   4

Electronic tuners are the best way to tune a guitar.

17

Exercise 7

Practice this quarter note exercise on the bottom three open strings.

Count: 1 2 3 4

Exercise 8

This exercise incorporates a wider variety of rhythms. Remember to play in time and keep an even tempo.

MINOR MELODY

Play the following with the band and use all six open strings. This tune will test how well you have learned to read all the open strings. When playing with the track, there is a four beat count off before you begin.

Chord symbols presented in songs are for accompaniment. These are also the chords used on the play along track.

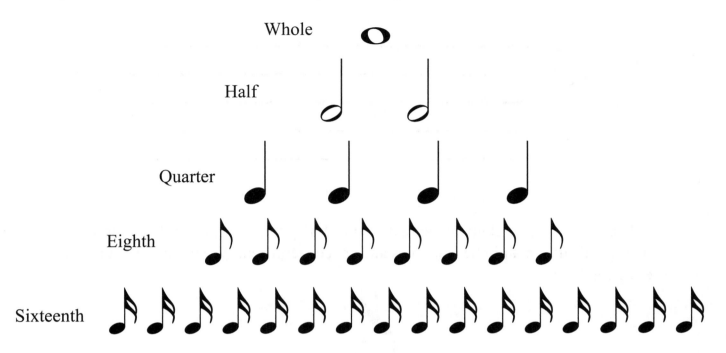

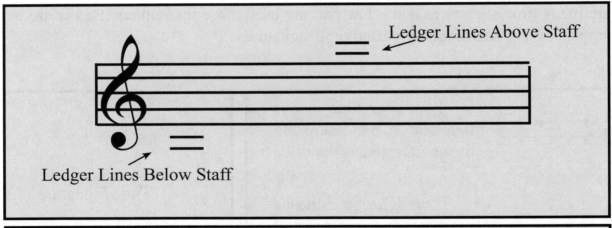

MAJOR SCALE MELODY

This song highlights the use of eighth notes and the C major scale. Practice slowly and evenly and then try playing with the band. Wait for the four beat count off to start.

STRAIGHT EIGHT BLUES

This is a 12 bar blues form. Play the eighth notes evenly. When you are able, try playing with the track on the CD. Wait for a four beat count off to start.

Whenever transporting a guitar, be sure and use a guitar case or gig bag.

NOTES ON THE 6TH STRING

Here are the notes we will learn on the 6th string. Work on memorizing them as you play the next few exercises.

E, OPEN 6TH STRING **F, 1ST FRET, 6TH STRING** **G, 3RD FRET, 6TH STRING**

Exercise 36

Practice this exercise playing whole notes.

Count: 1 2 3 4

Exercise 37

Practice this exercise playing half notes.

Count: 1 2 3 4

36

Exercise 38

Practice this exercise primarily playing quarter notes.

Count: 1 2 3 4

Exercise 39

This exercise uses a variety of rhythms. Practice smoothly and evenly.

1ST ENDING, 2ND ENDING

A first ending means to go back to the beginning of the tune or back to a repeat sign and play again. When we return to the first ending a second time, we skip the first ending and play the second ending which now completes the tune.

1st Ending   2nd Ending
1.   2.

3/4 TIME ARPEGGIOS

This song is in 3/4 time. It uses arpeggios or playing one note of a chord at a time. Practice playing with the band. This time there is a three beat count off.

THE E MINOR PENTATONIC SCALE

This is the E minor pentatonic scale. This scale is one of the most widely used scales on guitar. Practice it slowly at first and then work on speeding up.

 Songs

HOLD FOR TWO

This song uses the E minor pentatonic scale. It also highlights notes held for a long time. Make sure you continue to count while holding.

TIP *There are only 12 notes to play but there are an infinite amount of rhythms and dynamics.*

38

SECTION 4
SHARPS, FLATS, AND KEY SIGNATURES

CD1 51

THE SHARP

A sharp raises a note one fret. One fret higher or lower may also be called a half step. In the example below, we would play F sharp at the 2nd fret 1st string instead of F at the 1st fret 1st string. F sharp is said to be one half step higher than F (or one fret higher). Both sharps and flats are valid for one full measure.

This note is F sharp. It is played one fret higher than F (at the 2nd fret 1st string).

Sharp Sign

THE FLAT

A flat lowers a note one fret. One fret may also be called a half step. In the example below, we would play D flat at the 2nd fret 2nd string instead of D at the 3rd fret 2nd string. D flat is said to be one half step lower than D (or one fret lower)

This note is D flat. It is played one fret lower than D (at the second fret second string).

Flat Sign

THE NATURAL

A natural sign means the note is no longer flatted or sharped, but played at it's normal position. In the example below, the F sharp is no longer sharped when we see the natural sign and is played back at the 1st fret 1st string. Natural signs are necessary because sharp or flat signs are valid for one full measure. In other words, when a sharp or flat sign is presented in a measure, that note remains sharped or flatted for the rest of the measure unless otherwise indicated.

This note is F natural. It is played at it's usual place.

Natural Sign

40

Exercise 40

Practice this exercise observing the sharps. Follow the fingerings and they will help you play it smoothly and efficiently. Remember a sharp raises a note one half step or one fret higher.

Exercise 41

This exercise has sharps, flats, and naturals. Remember, once a note is sharped or flatted, it remains sharped or flatted throughout the measure unless a natural sign is introduced. A note is no longer sharped or flatted in the next measure unless it has another sharp or flat.

THE CHROMATIC SCALE

Chromatic means moving by half steps or one fret at a time. This chromatic scale is every note in the first position, one after the other. Play this scale slowly and evenly, paying close attention to the fingerings. This is a great exercise for using the 4th finger of the left hand.

TIP

The guitar was originally designed as a disposable instrument.

41

Exercise 42

This exercise will further your acquaintance with sharps and flats.

ACCIDENTAL BOOGIE

This song incorporates accidentals, which is another word for sharps and flats. Practice reading the chromatic tones and pay close attention to the fingerings as they will help you play smooth and efficient. When able, try playing with the band. Wait for a four beat count off to begin.

TIP *Scales are like the alphabet. What you do with them is what creates expression.*

42

DOTTED NOTES

A dotted note takes the note value (rhythm), and adds half of its value to it. In Example 1 we have a dotted half note. A half note lasts two beats. When it's dotted, we add half of it's value to it (2+1=3) and the note now lasts three beats. In Example 2 we have a dotted quarter note. A quarter note usually lasts one beat. Add half of it's value to it and it now lasts one and one half beats.

EXAMPLE 1

1   2   3   4

EXAMPLE 2

1   2   and   3   4

Exercise 43

This exercise highlights the use of dotted rhythms. Count carefully and pay attention to the ties. To help your counting, the beat that each note falls on is included above the staff. If you are unsure of the rhythms, listen to the audio example.

Exercise 44

This time watch the dotted quarter notes. Remember they last one and one half beats. To help you count, the beat that each note falls on is included above the staff. If you are unsure of the rhythms listen to the audio example.

TIP
A good strap should be connected to the guitar by a set of strap locks.

43

MAJORLY BLUE

Majorly Blue is a blues tune that incorporates accidentals, making it sound brighter.
When playing with the band, wait for a four beat count off to start.

CATALONIAN SONG

This famous folk song melody is in 3/4 time. Count 1 and 2 and 3 and, making
sure to observe the dotted rhythms. When able, try playing with the track. Wait for
the three beat count off to begin.

KEY SIGNATURES

A key signature tells us what notes are flatted or sharped throughout the tune. It's name also tells us what key we are in. In Example 1, the sharp is located on the top line where the note F would normally be played. This means that throughout this tune the note F, wherever it is found, (not just on the top line of the staff) is sharped unless otherwise indicated. This also tells us the song is in the key of G. The key of G has one sharp, F sharp, and this can be seen when playing a G major scale in Example 2.

Key Signature

EXAMPLE 1

The note F is sharped.

EXAMPLE 2: THE G MAJOR SCALE

This is in contrast to C major which has no sharps or flats in it. Look at Example 3 and 4.

Key Signature
(no sharps or flats)

EXAMPLE 3

EXAMPLE 4: THE C MAJOR SCALE

TIP
Never use furniture polish on your guitar.
Use guitar polish and a guitar cloth.

In Example 5, we have one flat in the key signature. This is located on the third line of the staff where the note B would normally be played. Because of this key signature, the note B will be flatted (one fret lower) throughout this tune or exercise. This is also the key of F which is seen in Example 6.

EXAMPLE 5

Key Signature

EXAMPLE 6: THE F MAJOR SCALE

1   3   1   3   2   3

The note B must be flatted

Exercise 45

This exercise highlights the use of the F sharp in the key signature (the key of G major). The note F must be sharped wherever it is found in this exercise.

3 2   3   3 1   2   3   3 2   3   3 1   2   3

4 2   2   3 2   2   4 2   2   3 2   2   4

Exercise 46

There is a B flat in the key signature of this exercise (the key of F major). Every B in this melody must be flatted. The B flat in measure 6 can be found at the 3rd fret 3rd string.

1   3   2   3 1   1   3   3   1   3 1 3   2   3

TIP

Never leave your guitar where it can get extremely hot or cold.

CARELESS LOVE

Careless Love is a well known traditional tune with a great melody. The key signature tells us we are in the key of G. This means every time you find the note F, you must sharp it and play F sharp. Try playing with the band. Wait for the four beat count off to start.

BOUREE

This is a classical melody written by Robert de Visee. Watch the B flat in the key signature and take note of the repeat sign at the end. In the full tune there is more to this melody (we are only playing the first half). When you can play this comfortably, try playing with the track. There will be a three beat count off before you start. It is only three counts because the first measure is a pick up. You must begin to play on beat four.

Note - This piece is a duet for two guitars. There are three tracks - Track 41 is the duet with both guitars, Track 42 is the 2nd guitar along with metronome, and Track 43 is the 2nd guitar by itself so you can practice or use in a student recital.

TIP *Solos are a combination of scales, arpeggios, licks, and expression.*

MINUET IN G

This is another classical melody and this time by J. S. Bach. This famous melody is presented in the key of G. Take note that it is in 3/4 time. In the full piece there is more to this melody (we are only playing the first half). Wait for the three beat count off to start playing with the accompaniment.

Note - This piece is a duet for two guitars. There are three tracks - Track 44 is the duet with both guitars, Track 45 is the 2nd guitar along with metronome, and Track 46 is the 2nd guitar by itself so you can practice or use in a student recital.

HIGH PEDAL IN G

This tune highlights the use of a high pedal tone on the open third string. Alternate your picking or finding the correct string to play will prove difficult. When playing with the band, wait for the four beat count off to start.

TIP *The Let's Jam CDs are great for practicing scales and licks.*

SECTION 5
HARMONY AND CHORDS

Playing more than one note at a time results in what is called harmony. Playing three or more notes at a time is generally going to be called a chord. Music notation tells us to play more than one note at a time by stacking the notes on top of each other in the same vertical space. Example 1 is an example of harmony. We are to play both the notes C and E at the same time. Example 2 is a series of harmonized notes. Example 3 is an example of a chord. We are to play all three notes: C, E, and G at the same time. This makes a C major chord or what is also called a triad.

EXAMPLE 1

EXAMPLE 2

EXAMPLE 3

Example 4 is a D major chord. Even though we are playing four strings at the same time, we are really only playing three different notes, D on the fourth string, A on the third string, another D on the second string, and the note F sharp on the first string. Take note of the F sharp in the key signature.

EXAMPLE 4

D

Example 5 is an E minor chord. We are playing all six strings at the same time but once again only three different notes. E on the 6th string, B on the 5th string, E on the 4th string, G on the 3rd string, B on the 2nd string, and E on the 1st string (E, G, B).

EXAMPLE 5

Em

TIP

When soloing, the goal is to create a melody. Hopefully create an interesting one.

50

CD1 62

Exercise 47

This exercise is a two note harmony with a low melody. The lower notes are written as eighth notes but let them ring as you play the higher notes. Play all of this exercise using downstrokes. Notice your first finger never has to leave the 1st fret 2nd string.

CD1 63

Exercise 48

This exercise has a three note harmony with a lower melody. Once again let all of the notes ring during this exercise. Notice the fingerings for the last chord (Em) are placed next to the notes they are to play. This is a common way to write fingerings when playing several notes at a time.

CD2 49-50 Songs

CHORD PLAY

The chord is first played as an arpeggio and then as a chord to be strummed. The first four notes of the measure create the chord. Leave the left fingers pressing down and let them ring to create the full chord. Notice the fingering below the staff.

Exercise 49

This is a chordal exercise. Use your note reading skills to identify the notes of each chord. The fingerings are presented the first time you see the chord but are omitted the next time. This tells the player to use the same fingerings the next time.

THE KEY OF D

The key of D has two sharps, F sharp and C sharp. When you see this key signature you must sharp every F and C sharp unless told otherwise.

Key Signature ⟶ **KEY OF D**

Exercise 50

This exercise is the D major scale. Remember to sharp any C or F you play.

D MELODY

This tune is in the key of D. Let the notes ring whenever possible. Wait for the four beat count off when playing with the track.

ARPEGGIATION

Here is another song in the key of D. These are arpeggios so let all the notes ring whenever possible. The trick to playing this type of tune is to visualize and make the whole chord at the start of each arpeggio. To help you get accustomed to this idea, the chord diagrams for each arpeggio are provided. As you progress, you will begin to identify these chords on your own. Pay close attention to the fingering and notice the descending D major scale in bar 8. When you are comfortable playing this tune try playing with the band. Wait for the four beat count off to begin.

TIP

When playing guitar, use the lightest touch possible on the fretboard that will get a clear note.

53

WAYFARING STRANGER

This well known melody is in E minor. E minor has the same key signature as G major. This is referred to as relative major and minor. G major and E minor are said to be relative because they both have only one sharp in the key signature (F sharp). Watch the ties and chord shapes while working on this tune. Take special note of the lower notes that are whole notes and ring while upper notes are played. The first time we see this is in the third measure. Keep these notes ringing and leave the fingers in place while you play the upper notes. When you are comfortable playing this tune, try playing with the band. There is a pick up at the beginning so you will come in on the second half of beat three. Count 1 and 2 and 3, coming in on the next "and" of the beat. This tune also works well as a solo piece.

TIP *A good teacher can dramatically increase your rate of learning.*

G BLUES

This blues in G highlights some great blues lines. Watch out for the accidentals and the challenging rhythms. When you are able, try playing with the band. Wait for the four beat count off to start.

PLAYING B IN TWO PLACES

We have been playing the note B on the middle line of the staff on the open 2nd string. We can also play this note on the 3rd string 4th fret. They are exactly the same note played on different strings. As you progress with your note reading and move up the guitar neck, you will find there are several places to play the same notes on the guitar. In order to play the next song, we will need to play the note B on the open 2nd string and at the 4th fret 3rd string.

THE NOTE B

This note may be played on the open second string or the 4th fret 3rd string. Play this note in both places and compare. They are the same.

Have your guitar set up twice a year. Once in the spring and once in the fall.

KEMP'S JIG

This tune is another famous folk melody. This is meant to be played as a solo piece so there is no accompanying track. This is a challenging tune to read so be patient and practice slowly. Notice the fingerings and the notes that are ringing while others are being played. Take special note of the first and second endings. The first ending repeat sign takes you back to the previous repeat sign (bar 9), not the beginning of the tune.

TIP For more scales try **The Guitarist's Scale Book** by Watch & Learn.

THE KEY OF E

The key signature for the key of E has four sharps, F sharp, C sharp, G sharp, and D sharp. Every F, C, G and D are to be sharped in this key unless told otherwise. At first this may be hard to keep track of, but with practice you will get used to this key. The key of E is an extremely common key for guitar so you must become comfortable reading and playing in this key.

Exercise 51

This exercise is the E major scale. Practice it until you can play it smoothly. Pay attention to the fingering, especially when you get to the note B in the middle of the staff. This note is to be played on the 3rd string 4th fret.

CASCADE IN E

This melody in E sounds best if you let the notes ring together in a cascading like sound. Keep an eye on the fingerings and take special note of the B in measure five which is played at the 4th fret 3rd string. When you are comfortable playing this tune, try playing with the band. Wait for the four beat count off to begin.

E BLUES DOUBLE STOPS

CD2 62-63 Songs

Double stops means to play two notes at once. It is another way to say harmony. Watch the accidentals and the rest bars. Once you are able, try playing with the band. Wait for the four beat count off to start.

CONGRATULATIONS!

You have now completed *Guitar Method 1* by *Watch & Learn*. You may want to try our other guitar products like *The Guitarist's Scale Book* or *The Guitarist's Chord Book*. If you are looking to increase your music theory knowledge try *The Guitarist's Music Theory Book*. Courses like *Introduction to Blues Guitar* or *Introduction to Rock Guitar* would be a great way to increase your guitar playing abilities as well. If acoustic guitar playing is your style try the *Acoustic Rock Guitar Primer*.

Wherever you go from here, we hope you have increased your knowledge and enjoyment of the guitar. Once again, congratulations on finishing this course.

TIP *To change strings, you should have a set of wire cutters and a peg winder.*